Business Ideas for the Future Autistic Business Owner
Dawn Lucan

Business Ideas for the Future Autistic Business Owner
© 2014 Dawn Lucan. All rights reserved
ISBN 978-1-312-25629-3

Table of Contents

Introduction
Creative Side
Culinary Arts
Neighborhood Jobs
Technology
Resources

Introduction

I have been a small business owner since 2008 when I first started writing books on Special Education. I was not new to working for a small business in life since I have worked in the past for my father. I have also worked for big business at times in the past. I noticed over time that I was not in control over my destiny, and I began searching for ways to create a steady income stream for myself.

Running a business can be quite consuming depending on the type of business you chose to start. Some businesses take very little money to start it, but they can be quite time consuming. While other businesses take a lot of money to start it. I recommend before you start your own small business that you research it before you start it.

You are not alone out there in starting a small business because others have done it in the past. There is help out there for you to start your own business through the government and banks. Mentors are available for free to guide you through the steps.

I pay Social Security and income taxes based on my royalties. The federal income tax comes out of my royalty check even before I see it, and I do not mind at all. I never mind paying my Social Security taxes because it will benefit me when I retire in life. We all benefit as a society from paying our taxes in services.

I know you can do it with the right mentoring along with your family and friends. I have included some great resources for you to help your business with great tools.

I recommend go for your business dreams in life. If everything goes right for you with your business, you will enjoy every single minute of running it. I also know from personal experience that if you dream it that things can happen for you, too.

Dawn Lucan

Creative Side

Artist

An artist is great at drawing or painting places, people, or objects. They can make the painting or drawing come alive in so many different ways for their audience. Artists can sell their drawings and paintings through craft shows and art galleries.

Resources
www.cafepress.com
www.etsy.com

Author

If you are great at writing, you might want to consider becoming an author. You can do this through writing magazine articles or books. It can be difficult to become well known as an author, and I have even seen famous people who wrote a book that could not sell many books. For magazines, you would get paid by the word so many cents per word. For books, you would get paid per book sold.

Resource
www.lulu.com

Candlemaker

Candles are the earliest forms of lights used in households and businesses by individuals. Today, they are now used for special occasions. The candles come in scented and unscented forms. They are easy to make with very simple ingredients found in any craft supply store. These can be sold on the web, farmers market, flea market, or craft show.

Resource
www.etsy.com

Clown

If you love goofing off and showing off for a crowd, you will love being a clown in life. Clowns are expected to do several different performances in front of a crowd such as doing balloon tricks. You can perform at children's parties, nonprofit events, and more. I recommend having a set rate, but I do recommend being flexible on pay.

Comedian

If you are really great at humor and telling jokes, you could become a comedian. The best comedians know how to turn daily life into humor with the audience. You can start out small with your local community before you try a larger audience outside of it to develop your trade. It does take time to get established in this job, so I recommend you having another job while trying to get established into it.

Comic Book Author

If you are good at telling a story through drawings and writing, you might want to consider becoming a comic book author. You first create a story broken down into easy to digest bits. Then, you come up with the pictures to match the story. Finally, you write the dialogue to go along with the pictures. You can do this as an independent through a publisher and set your own prices.

Resources
www.cafepress.com
www.lulu.com

Crafts

There are crafts people out there who sell their items at craft sales and even over the internet. It is a tough market to get into unfortunately. It takes a lot of practice and skill to sell anything in this market. You can sell your items on the internet, your local craft shows, or craft fairs. Depending on your local community, there are some stores that sell crafts. It also takes a little bit of money to develop your product with enough samples to sell. You can sell your products on the web and craft shows.

Resource
www.etsy.com

DJ

You could become a DJ if you have an ear for music and know how to put great songs together. It takes a lot of money to put together the equipment to make it work besides getting a song list. You have to have a large number of songs available to attract clients. It does take time to get established in the business, so I recommend having another job when you start in it.

Illustrator

An illustrator is someone who loves to draw for a special cause such as a children's book, greeting cards, magazines, posters, etc. They turn words into beautiful pictures to go with words in a book. It can be a difficult market to get into depending on your talent. However, it does pay well per project. I recommend using guru.com and cafepress.com for this business type.

Resources
www.cafepress.com
www.etsy.com

Jewelry Designer

If you love to string beads, you could design and create your own jewelry line. People are always looking for unique jewelry to wear each day. You can find your supplies at the local craft store. You can sell your jewelry at the local craft fair, flea market, and online store.

Resource
www.etsy.com

Magician

If you love performing magic tricks, it can turn into a great career for you. The tricks do not need expensive equipment or complex tricks. You can even perform in your local community and the surrounding area to do it. Parents are always looking for a magician to perform at a child's birthday party. You can also perform at meetings and local community events. You can set your own rate for it or you can negotiate with the parents based on their own budget.

Photographer

If you love taking pictures through your camera, you can become a photographer. You can take pictures of individuals through portraits, special events, landscapes, and more. You can even put together your pictures through a calendar and sell the calendars. You can sell your products on the web, flea markets, and craft fairs. I also recommend using Cafepress.com for this business.

Resources
www.cafepress.com
www.etsy.com

Tshirt Designer

Tshirt designers combine their love of graphics with a passion for clothing. They come up with images and/or sayings to place on their clothing to sell to people. You can paint your images onto the tshirt or you can press the design onto the tshirt. You can get your supplies at the local craft store. You can sell your shirts online, flea markets, and craft fairs.

Resources
www.cafepress.com
www.etsy.com

Videographer

A videographer is someone who video tapes special events for someone else and gets paid for it. It can be for a family's special event to corporate events. You can determine what field you specialize in for your local community. There is at least several events happening every day in your local community that needs a videographer. You do need your own video camera, computer, DVD burner, and specialized software to do it. You do not need a college education in most cases. However, I do recommend creating a web page and learning about running a business.

Resources
www.bbb.org
www.sba.gov
www.score.org
www.uschamber.com

Culinary Arts

Baker

A baker is someone who loves to create breads, rolls, cakes, and cupcakes. You can open your own bakery or do it at home depending on your town's regulations. It just takes following the directions through a recipe and baking it for a certain length of time. I recommend taking a cooking class in high school or at your local community college through their continuing education department. You can sell your baked goods at flea markets, craft shows, and farmer markets.

Chocolate Maker

Almost everyone enjoys candy and especially chocolate. It is relatively simple to make. You can be as creative as you want with the ingredients added into your chocolate candies. You can find the ingredients in any store. You can sell your chocolates at farmer's markets, fairs, flea markets, and craft shows.

Food Vendor

At sporting events, fairs, craft shows, and more, you see people selling food to attendees. They make money off of what they sell. They sell popular food items such as popcorn, hot dogs, water, soda, and more. They purchase their food items at a warehouse for discounted prices in bulk, and they mark it up at the event to make a profit.

Personal Chef

If you love to cook meals, you might want to become a personal chef for a family. You could be cooking ahead meals for the week for a family for them to reheat at a later time. At times, you could also be preparing food for a dinner party for a couple and their friends. You would be working with the family to plan a menu for that period of time before you delivered your product. You could set your own price, or you would work out a price per meal or week with the family.

Neighborhood Jobs

Babysitter

Do you love caring for children? You can care for children at their home or your home for money. You would only need training from the American Red Cross in babysitting along with CPR and first aid training. The hours and pay would be dependent on the family that you babysit their children on a regular basis.

Resources
www.care.com
www.sittercity.com

Dog Walker

Do you enjoy being around pets or especially dogs? You should consider becoming a dog walker. You would be taking care of a dog for a certain number of minutes each day for someone while they were not at home for either travel or work. The pay is not much, so I recommend keeping to clients in your neighborhood.

Resource
www.care.com

Housecleaner

If you love to clean or good at it, there are always people looking for someone to clean their house for pay. It would be either like once a week or every other week depending on the needs of the family. You can schedule the day of the week based on your needs. However, the pay is dependent upon you negotiating with the family. You can post this on the supermarket advertisement wall or online.

Resource
www.care.com

Lawnmower

Do you enjoy lawnmowers or taking care of grass? I recommend becoming a lawnmower. In most parts of the world, this is a seasonal job. However, there are people willing to pay for someone to do this household chore instead of themselves. I recommend using clients in your own neighborhood due to the low pay.

Mother's Helper

Once in a while, I will spot an advertisement for a mother's helper. You would be helping with various tasks around the house or caring for the children to make the parents' lives easier. You would be working a set of given hours a day. The pay is based on what you and the parents agree on at the time you start.

Resource
www.care.com

Professional Organizer

You have loved organizing things since you were very young. You would organize your toy trucks in a row. Did you know that you can get paid for organizing someone else's life? It could be as small as organizing the person's closet to organizing a whole house. It would include organizing things into storage containers.

Snow Shoveling

If you live in a place where you get a lot of snow, snow shoveling can bring in a lot of money depending on the homeowner. It depends on how much show has fallen besides the length of sidewalk and driveway involved. For this career, I recommend sticking to your own neighborhood to save money on gas with your clients.

Tutor

Parents are always looking for help for their children in their weak subjects at school. If you are strong in a particular subject, you could become a tutor. You could even tutor people how to use a computer. I recommend tutoring someone in your neighborhood or close by because your pay depends on the family.

Resource
www.care.com

Technology

App Programmer

If you are good at programming a computer, you might enjoy creating programs for computer or cell phone applications. People are always looking for the perfect computer or cell phone program to enhance their life. They are willing to pay good money for it, but I caution you to research prices of similar programs before you set your price. You would get a royalty from each sale.

Computer Repair

Computers are an expensive investment for a family even at today's prices. They either get a computer virus, want to install a new program, or upgrade their computer. Most individuals do not know how to do these things themselves and require help. With some courses taken at your local community college or technical high school, you can start your own business in computer repair.

Webmaster

A webmaster is someone who creates web pages for a living for someone else. You could create web pages for an individual, nonprofit, or business. Each page has its own challenges in creating it to match the specific customer's needs. You do not need a college education to get started. There are some good books on creating a web page at your local bookstore or public library.

Resources
www.coffeecup.com
www.ineedhits.com
www.tys.us

Website Marketing

If you know a particular type of business well or several, you might want to get into website marketing. Businesses are often too busy to do it themselves and are looking for someone to promote their business over the web. It could be as simple as keeping a blog on Facebook.com or keyword search results on a search engine such as Google.com or Yahoo.com. Before you start this business, I recommend reading some books on it at your local library or at the bookstore.

Resources
www.facebook.com
www.ineedhits.com

Resources

I have put together a list of great general resources to help you start your own business.

www.cafepress.com
www.care.com
www.coffeecup.com
www.elance.com
www.etsy.com
www.facebook.com
www.fbo.gov
www.gofundme.com
www.guru.com
www.ineedhits.com
www.irs.gov
www.linkedin.com
www.lulu.com
www.paypal.com
www.prweb.com
www.sba.gov
www.score.org
www.sittercity.com
www.ssa.gov
www.twitter.com
www.tys.us
www.vistaprint.com

www.ingramcontent.com/pod-product-compliance
Lightning Source LLC
Chambersburg PA
CBHW081145170526
45158CB00009BA/2684